GRAND CANYON
WILD

Grand Canyon Wild

A Photographic Journey

John Annerino

The Countryman Press

Woodstock, Vermont

Photographs and essays © 2004 by John Annerino

First Edition

All rights reserved.

Library of Congress Cataloging-in-Publication Data
Annerino, John.
    Grand Canyon wild : a photographic journey / John Annerino. —1st ed.
      p. cm.
   ISBN 0-88150-593-5
 1. Grand Canyon (Ariz.)—Description and travel. 2. Grand Canyon
(Ariz.)—Pictorial works. 3. Annerino, John—Travel—Arizona—Grand
Canyon. I. Title.

  F788.A6 2004
  917.91'32—dc22

                                     2004045535

Book design by Susan McClellan

Published by The Countryman Press,
P.O. Box 748, Woodstock, Vermont 05091

Distributed by W.W. Norton & Company, Inc.,
500 Fifth Avenue, New York, NY 10110

Printed in Spain by Artes Graficas Toledo

10 9 8 7 6 5 4 3 2 1

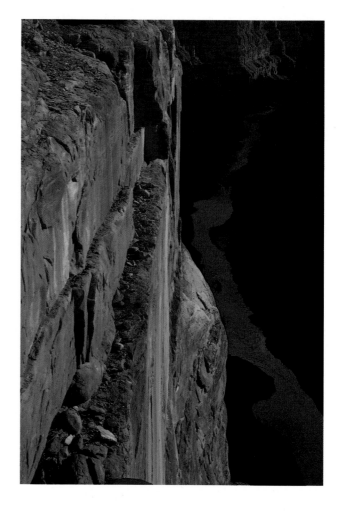

Toroweap Point, North Rim

For my sons,
follow your heart and
seek a good path in life.
For my wife and *mi vida*,
the bravest person I know.

Alpine lake, Little Colorado River headwaters

BOOKS BY JOHN ANNERINO

Photography

ROUGHSTOCK: The Toughest Events in Rodeo

APACHE: The Sacred Path to Womanhood

PEOPLE OF LEGEND: Native Americans of the Southwest

THE WILD COUNTRY OF MEXICO:
   La tierra salvaje de México

CANYONS OF THE SOUTHWEST

HIGH RISK PHOTOGRAPHY: The Adventure
   Behind the Image

Also by the author

RUNNING WILD: An Extraordinary Adventure from the
   Spiritual World of Running

DEAD IN THEIR TRACKS: Crossing America's Desert
   Borderlands

Stone face, Paria Canyon

I N THE GRAND CANYON, ARIZONA HAS A
natural wonder which, so far as I know, is
in kind absolutely unparalleled throughout the rest of the
world. I want to ask you to do one thing in connection with it
in your own interest and in the interest of the country—to keep
this great wonder of nature as it now is . . . I hope you will not
have a building of any kind, not a summer cottage, a hotel or
anything else, to mar the wonderful grandeur, the sublimity, the
great loveliness and beauty of the Canyon. Leave it as it is. You
cannot improve on it. The ages have been at work on it, and
man can only mar it. What you can do
is to keep it for your children, your children's
children, and for all who come after you, as the
one great sight which every American . . .
should see.

—President Theodore Roosevelt,
in a speech at the Grand Canyon, 1903

Stone Creek Falls, Middle Granite Gorge

ACKNOWLEDGMENTS

I'M GRATEFUL TO THE MANY PEOPLE who supported my quest to explore the Grand Canyon: Galen Snell, Craig Spillman, Chris May, Tim Ganey, Craig Hudson, Virginia Taylor, Dave Ganci, Christine Keith, Tony Mangine, Richard Nebeker, Kimmie Johnson, George Bain, Craig Newman, Suzanne Jordan, Robb Elliott, Martha Clark, Louise Teal, Tony Ebarb, and Melvin L. Scott. I'm also grateful for the expertise of Jim Fisher, Tim Miller, Esther Meyer, Jennifer Thompson, Susan McClellan, Richard Fumosa, and Jacques Chazaud in the pre-production, edit, design, and cartography of this book.

I laud the efforts of backcountry, river, rescue, interpretive, and law-enforcement rangers who work grueling hours to keep visitors safe and informed. I remain inspired by the Grand Canyon's first environmentalists: the Paiute, Havasupai, Hualapai, Hopi, and Navajo. At a time when this World Heritage site is threatened on many fronts, Grand Canyon lovers everywhere should listen to the words and study the traditions of the Grand Canyon's original stewards.

This lifelong dream would not have become a reality without Bill Rusin and Kermit Hummel. Thank you.

Sunbeam,
Antelope Canyon

CONTENTS

Sunset, Toroweap Point

INTRODUCTION

It is a region more difficult to traverse than the Alps or the Himalayas.
—Major John Wesley Powell, 1895, *Canyons of the Colorado*

I TOOK MY FIRST PHOTOGRAPH OF THE GRAND CANYON twenty-one years ago. I hadn't set out to photograph *the Canyon*, as I came to know it. At the time, I was leading a group of teens on a weeklong sojourn through the alpine forests of the North Rim. Wisps of clouds clung to the treetops when the afternoon rain finally broke. We strolled from our soggy camp toward the edge of the misty rim and peered into the evergreen depths of Crystal Creek. To our surprise twin rainbows arced over Dragon's Head, a rugged butte covered with a lush pelt of pine and fir. Shrouded in blue light that hummed with electricity, we were no longer at the Grand Canyon, we were in another time and another place. A battered Nikon dangled around my neck— I carried it to photograph my students. But instead of capturing their expressions of wonder, I framed the delicate sunbows plunging over the rim before us.

That moment changed me forever.

I gave up a decade-long career teaching outdoor education to pursue my gnawing passion for photography. But I still hadn't set out to photograph the Grand Canyon. Not yet.

A year later, a friend and I were standing on the edge of the South Rim. We'd just climbed out of the Canyon after a long trek across a hanging terrace called the Tonto Platform. We hadn't seen anyone else for fourteen hours. A warm breeze wicked the sweat off our salt-rimed faces. It was pitch-black and you couldn't see ten feet into the Canyon. A station wagon pulled up. A woman jumped out and left the motor running. She pointed a plastic Instamatic at the black hole. A pinprick of light went off. Turning to her husband and children, she announced, "I got it." She then drove off—the children's faces still pressed against the windows. I looked at my friend in disbelief.

It wasn't until days later that I realized I'd had a second decisive moment at the Canyon. Sitting in my cabin in Prescott, staring into the yellow flames of the potbellied stove, I started to wonder: "How *do* you photograph the Grand Canyon?" I could set up my tripod at a dozen different scenic vistas, but even in the best of conditions, I'd be taking the same photographs millions of others had taken before me.

John K. "Jack" Hillers, Chief Photographer for the U.S.

Twin rainbows, Dragon Head, North Rim

Geological Survey, had set the stage when he visited the North Rim with Major John Wesley Powell in 1872 and took the first photograph from Toroweap Point. It is one of the most remote and breathtaking vistas in North America. The first and last time I photographed the Canyon from Toroweap Point, twelve other photographers were jostling for position on Hillers's perch trying to take the same memorable image he'd shot 131 years earlier.

That wouldn't do.

A passage from Major Powell's *The Exploration of the Colorado River and Its Canyons* later steered me into the Grand Canyon to seek my own vision of it:

> *You cannot see the Grand Canyon in one view, as if it were a changeless spectacle from which a curtain might be lifted, but to see it you have to toil from month to month through its labyrinths. It is a region more difficult to traverse than the Alps or the Himalayas, but if strength and courage are sufficient for the task, by a year's toil a concept of sublimity can be obtained never again to be equaled on the hither side of Paradise.*

I didn't know if the Grand Canyon was more difficult to traverse than the Himalayas or the Alps, but I was hungry to see what lay beyond the all-too-familiar calendar scenes, coffee table views, and picture-postcard images taken from the Canyon's most frequented scenic overlooks. To do that I entered what at the time was a mysterious realm, seldom seen, little known, and rarely visit-ed; today five million visitors come from all over the world to pay homage to this natural wonder each year. Drawn by the quests of explorers, prospectors, surveyors, river runners, climbers, and Native Americans who forged the Grand Canyon's remarkable history, I spent years exploring the Canyon by foot, raft, and rope before the seed for this book first took.

Following ancient Indian routes and the historic trails of Spanish padres and Mormon missionaries, I traversed the horizons that lay beyond official national park boundaries, hoping to see how these men may have viewed the strange and wonderful land-marks that encircled the Grand Canyon. I traced the precarious routes of ancient Pueblo peoples to remote summits, like Shiva Temple, hoping to see the rim views that may have greeted them before the written word reached their world. I followed the Salt Trail of the Hopi Sun clan down the rugged Little Colorado River Gorge hoping to see the chasm views that dwarfed them during their sacred journeys. And I paddled and rowed the Colorado River hoping to see the river views that mesmerized the colorful cast of white-water adventurers who challenged its legendary rapids.

These were some of the stone corridors, desert trails, and windy summits I sought in search of adventure, calm, and images that said to me: "This is the Grand Canyon."

This is the Grand Canyon that enriched my life and shaped my vision. And this is the Grand Canyon I want to share with you.

Sit back, put your feet up, and marvel at the greatest canyon on earth.

Navajo Tribal Park, Yéii Bicheii Spires, Monument Valley

I. HORIZONS

GRAND CANYON COUNTRY

Sweeping back from the rimlands... a thousand
other landmarks spread throughout Grand Canyon country belong
to a rare land where the air is clear, and the people are few,
where the earth is nearly naked and the desert is painted.
—C. Gregory Crampton, 1972, *Land of Living Rock*

I'M DRAWN TO THE MYSTERIES OF THE CANYON'S GEOLOGY, the miracles of its biogeography, and the splendor of its flora and fauna. Yet, what often fascinates me most is its dramatic human landscape. Who struggled through the burning sands of the Desierto Pintado, or the deep snowdrifts of Buckskin Mountain, in order to reach the Grand Canyon; who avoided the "horrible abyss" at all costs; who staved off starvation by dining on the wretched meat of a raven; who slaked mad thirst by pressing cracked lips to shimmering pools of sweet rainwater? What landforms left the most indelible impressions on those who journeyed through Grand Canyon country before the automobile?

Probing the landscape with camera and pen, by foot and a hearty little truck that's never failed, I traced the overland routes of those who, with horseshoes and wagon wheels, ground the red rock and sagebrush to dust. In reading their journals, reaching the rim of the Canyon, or avoiding it, was rarely easy. Yet, it was always hauntingly beautiful because the Grand Canyon was the heart of the Colorado Plateau. A great multitiered landmass 6,000 feet high and 130,000 miles square, the Colorado Plateau overlaps the Four Corners region, where the state borders of Utah, Arizona, Colorado, and New Mexico meet. The Colorado River and its tributaries, including the Green, San Juan, Río Virgen, and Paria Rivers, are its lifeblood. They cut the plateau's deep labyrinths, in area that we know of today as the Narrows of Zion National Park, Horseshoe Bend of Canyonlands National Park, and the slot canyons of Paria Canyon Wilderness. They nurtured its native people who wrested a hardscrabble living in the stony barrens of Hovenweap National Monument and the piñon tree–covered tablelands of Mesa Verde National Park. Wind, rain, and ice carved soaring windows of stone in Arches National Park, flaming red spires in Monument Valley Navajo Tribal Park, and impregnable walls in Vermilion Cliffs National Monument. In between, sweeping deserts created blank spots on the maps with death traps that bore descriptive names like Great Basin, Painted, and Sonoran. Majestic to behold, the harsh character of this raw, untamed land lay bare, and it both lured and defied all comers.

Dawn, Dead Horse Point State Park

Many stories of traversing the desolate plateau lands resonate with me. Some journeys brought undeniable hardships, others simple joy. Lay a wooden pencil in the middle of a Grand Canyon map, about where the Dutch-born American geologist François-Emile Matthes created a topographic work of art in 1905 called *Bright Angel*, and flick it with your finger. Before it stops spinning, you'll follow the route of Mormon missionary Jacob Hamblin who became the first to travel all the way around the Grand Canyon in 1862; riding a mule in quest of souls, the "Buckskin Apostle" covered five hundred miles in sixty days. If the pencil tip points southeast, you can trace the route of García López de Cárdenas across the Painted Desert to the South Rim; led by Hopi guides, the conquistador "discovered" the Grand Canyon in 1540. When the tip points southwest, you can follow the route of Francisco Tómas Garcés from the Mojave Desert to Havasu Canyon; that's where the Spanish missionary became the first European to descend into the Grand Canyon in 1776. If the tip points north, you can follow the route of Francisco Atanasio Domínguez and Silvestre Vélez de Escalante beneath the imposing walls of Vermilion Cliffs; the Spanish explorers desperately searched for a route out of Grand Canyon country four months after Padre Garcés had found a way into it.

The adventures, discoveries, and revelations of these explorers captivated me. So did Major Powell's 1872 overland journey from the "dark and gloomy" depths of Zion Narrows to the yawning brink of Toroweap Point. What touched me most was Powell's admiration for the Kaibab Paiute who guided him through their ancestral canyon lands: "These Indians put me to shame," Powell wrote. "They know every rock and ledge, every gulch and cañon . . . and their knowledge is unerring."

Yet, one journey across the Canyon's horizon has stood out for me. In 1884, Charles F. Lummis set out on a 3,507-mile near-transcontinental walk from Cincinnati to Los Angeles. Lummis had two motives. He had accepted a job offer as an editor for the *Los Angeles Times*, and he was determined to see the country. In *A Tramp Across the Continent*, Lummis wrote: "Railroads and Pullmans were invented to help us hurry through life . . . I am a American and feel ashamed to know so little about my country as I do."

I had no intention of walking, or even driving, from Cincinnati to Los Angeles to follow Lummis's route. But he inspired me to climb a daunting canyon perch with a friend. While chasing a deer in the Painted Desert, Lummis broke his arm. Far from medical help, he treated the shattered bones himself. In spite of the pain, Lummis and his dog detoured from their epic tramp and hiked down Peach Springs Canyon "to visit the greatest wonder in the world—the Grand Cañon of the Colorado."

That's where I picked up his trail. Even with two good hands, I was unnerved following Lummis's route two thousand feet up a pyramid of crumbly stone to a summit view of Grand Canyon country that described my own: "The wild majestic cliffs loomed taller, nobler, more marvelous." Indeed, they did.

Twilight, Delicate Arch, Arches National Park

Moonrise, Cliff Palace,
Mesa Verde National Park

ABOVE: Rock mushrooms, Canyonlands National Park
RIGHT: Daybreak, Mesa Arch, Canyonlands National Park

Moonrise, Hovenweap Castle, Hovenweap National Monument

Square Tower House,
Mesa Verde National Park

Sunrise, (left to right)
West Mitten Butte,
Sentinel Mesa, and
Big Indian

Fallen timbers, West Fork, Oak Creek

Frijoles Falls, Bandelier
National Monument

27

Sunset, southern
escarpment, Colorado
Plateau

LEFT: Merrick Butte, Monument Valley
ABOVE: Forested canyon, West Fork, Oak Creek

ABOVE: Caprock hoodoo, Grand Staircase–Escalante National Monument

RIGHT: Red Rock Country, Colorado Plateau

OVERLEAF: Summer monsoon, Canyonlands National Park

II. RIMS

OVER THE EDGE

Overlooking the most wonderful scenery in the world.

The moon was full. Dim, vast, mysterious, the canyon

lay in the shimmering radiance.

—Theodore Roosevelt, 1916,

A Book-Lover's Holidays in the Open

I FIRST HEARD THE CALL OF THE GRAND CANYON IN MY early twenties. A professor told me I must see the Canyon. I ignored him because I was pulled in other directions. The Chiricahua Mountains, mythic redoubt of Cochise and Geronimo. The Superstition Mountains, fabled hideaway of the Lost Dutchman's Gold. The San Francisco Mountains, sacred abode of Hopi and Navajo deities. How could any canyon compare? Finally, my professor invited me on a weekend hike down the Boucher Trail. It became my favorite. And I led others down the narrow, rocky path that clung to the edge of canyon walls where one misstep could be the last.

We don't know how the Anaasází viewed the Canyon. And we may never know. They were phantoms. But when they peered over the edge of their world, they found a way down to the silver water that snaked through the black rocks far below. It was not an easy journey. Wearing flimsy yucca-fiber sandals where I wore sturdy leather boots, they picked their way through tremendous cliffs, past nests of golden eagles, at times clinging by their fingertips to flesh-ripping limestone, until they could walk upright once more. Children in tow, they carried their burden of water in deerskins, their rations of sundried meat, agave hearts, and piñón nuts in baskets suspended by trump lines. Following hidden ledges and hanging canyons, through frightening precipices that date back 1.7 billion years, they descended a mile-deep chasm of puzzling escarpments that others would name Kaibab, Toroweap, Coconino, Hermit, Supai, Redwall, Bright Angel, Muav, Tapeats, and Vishnu. Quenching their thirst in the waters of the Colorado River, they knew their precarious route had linked the deep desert with their lofty woodlands. Thus began their seasonal migrations, their tilling of plots of corn, beans, and squash along the river during winter, hunting and gathering of native foods on the rim during summer. This tough life and meager living came to a mysterious end circa A.D. 1150 when the Anaasází abandoned the Grand Canyon. No one knows why. But they left behind four thousand stone dwellings they'd once called home, and a network of cliff-hugging passages that others would follow.

McKee Point, South Rim

The trail I followed along the rimrock that warm spring day was hand-hewn along an Anaasází path by Louis D. Boucher. A French Canadian by birth, Boucher heard the wild tales of the Canyon's treasures, and in 1891 he came to the South Rim in search of his. A hermit who "wore a white beard and white mustache [while] jogging along on his white mule," Boucher was one of many prospectors who hoped to hit pay dirt during the 1880s and '90s. Digging, hacking, and blasting trails into the depths of the Canyon, they came in search of copper, silver, and gold. Some trails even bore their names: Bass, for William Wallace; Hance, for "Captain" John; and Tanner, for Seth B. But hitting the mother lode in the Grand Canyon, most discovered, was a bust. For some it proved to be a "granite prison," and the last place they should have ever tread. Those who stayed behind, like Bass and Hance, pocketed more "color"-guiding tinhorns into the Canyon than hauling out burro loads of low-grade ore.

Of the eighty-four trails miners chiseled through the Canyon's rainbow of stone, none is more storied in Grand Canyon country than the Tanner Trail. Devoid of water and exposed to the broiling sun, few were as dangerous. The first time I traced the steep, faint path, I put my ear to the ground and listened to its voices. I listened to the screams of Navajo fleeing Colonel Christopher "Kit" Carson's scorched-earth campaign of 1863. I listened to the chants of medicine men singing sacred words of power in order to protect them from Carson's reach: "Enemies that shall die, Of the Coyote that shall eat them, Of the crow that shall eat them . . ." I listened to the whispers of rustlers who stole horses in Flagstaff and switched brands on the Tanner Trail before riding back to Utah. I listened to the words of Bass, who rode the Tanner Trail searching for John D. Lee's hidden bonanza of "seven cans of almost pure native gold."

At day's end, I camped in the warm sand at the foot of the old Indian trail, and I listened to the music of the great river as a full moon climbed over the black wall of Comanche Point. Canyon names drifted by in the river's song: Shiva, Deva, Brahma, temples named after Eastern deities by Clarence E. Dutton during the 1880s—because the pillars of stone were too sublime to be named after mere mortals. He was right. Old West cowhands had a saying for rough-cut country like this: "It's a helluva place to lose a cow." It was a heck of a place to swim a herd of deer across the Colorado River, too. But that's exactly what a hundred cowboys and Indians tried to do in 1924. After rounding up "5,000 to 10,000" mule deer on the North Rim to reduce the herd, they'd push them down the Horsethief Trail, then out the Tanner Trail to the South Rim, collecting $2.50 a head. The preposterousness of the failed scheme awakened me. I looked up from my sleeping bag and listened to a Rough Rider's poetry echo across the rim far above: "The moon was full. Dim, vast, mysterious, the canyon lay in the shimmering radiance." Moon, river, and dreams soothed me back to sleep.

Standing on the edge, Shiva Temple

The Colorado from Toroweap Point

Rockslide, western Grand Canyon

The Colorado,
Lava Falls

Sunset, the Colorado, near Shivwits Crossing

Tyrolean traverse, Thunder River

Marble Canyon, the Colorado
at Four Mile Wash

45

ABOVE: Daybreak, East Rim, Vermilion Cliffs National Monument
CENTER: Tooth Rock, East Rim, Vermilion Cliffs National Monument

ABOVE: **Sundown, Echo Cliffs**

OPPOSITE: **Balanced Rock, Glen Canyon, Lees Ferry**   ABOVE: **Horseshoe Bend, the Colorado at Nine Mile Bar**

First light, Angels Gate

Rappeling, Angels Gate

51

Skies of fire,
Aubrey Cliffs

ABOVE: **The Redwall below McKee Point** RIGHT: **The Redwall, Honga Springs**

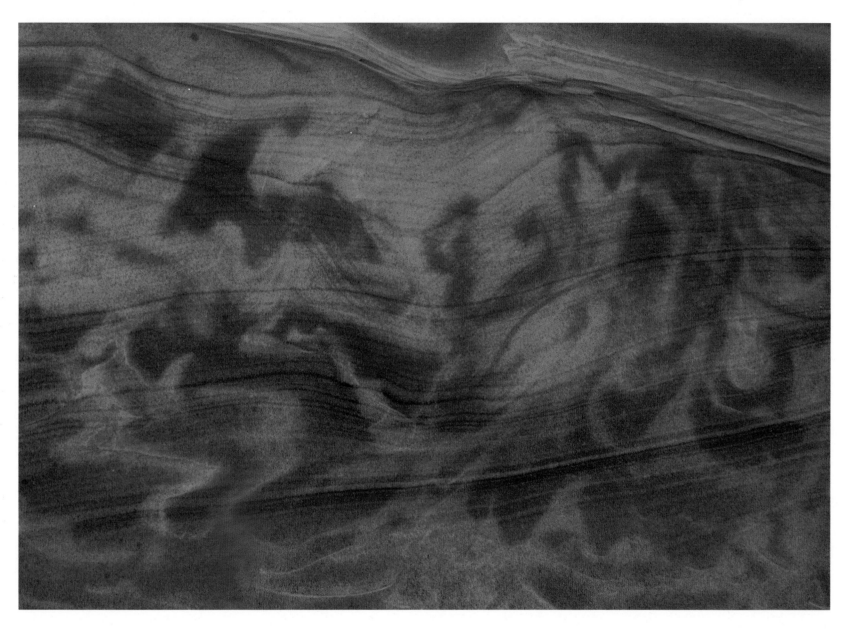

Petrified sand dunes, Paria Canyon–Vermilion Cliffs Wilderness

OPPOSITE: **Wildfire sunset, Cape Royal**   ABOVE: **Petrified sand dunes, Paria Canyon–Vermilion Cliffs Wilderness**

Nightfall, East Rim, Vermilion Cliffs
National Monument

A climber's view,
Peach Springs Canyon

ABOVE: Climber, southwest face, Zoroaster Temple

RIGHT: Twilight, Thor Temple

LEFT: **Storm, Vishnu Temple**   ABOVE: **Staring into an abyss, Shiva Temple**

ABOVE: Rappeling, Comanche Point   RIGHT: Comanche Point, Palisades of the Desert

III. CHASMS
MYSTERIES OF THE DEEP

I looked into the canyon, which seemed miles deep,
and saw the Little Colorado River shining from the bottom.
I was frightened and wondered if we would ever return safely.
—Don C. Talayesva, 1912,
Sun Chief: The Autobiography of a Hopi Indian

I WAS IN HIGH-SCHOOL GEOGRAPHY CLASS THE FIRST TIME I studied a map. The teacher bored me, but the map hanging over the blackboard behind him was a passport for my imagination. Sitting at my desk, I could travel anywhere on flights of fancy. Years later, those journeys became more focused. At home, I'd spread my map across the kitchen table, look at the deep gashes in the earth and wonder what it'd be like to follow a drop of water from the tortured escarpments of the high plateaus to the mother river of the Colorado. In reality, I've done that many times since, because a labyrinth of stone corridors feeds the Colorado River on its serpentine, three-hundred-mile course between the ruby alcoves of Glen Canyon and the somber abyss of Black Canyon.

I traced my finger across the map one night, and peered down at Antelope Canyon. It wasn't the Colorado River's longest or deepest tributary, but its fossilized waves of golden stone formed one of the most beautiful canyons in the world. The story of its discovery was no less bewitching. Imagine a sunbeam shining down on an angelic, black-haired girl, dressed in a turquoise skirt, silver-buttoned blouse, and moccasins, leading a flock of bleating white sheep through a cathedral of stone.

Though it was a landscape that drove many pioneers to privation, exhaustion, and forlorn headstones, the beauty of Navajo legend captivated me. I made the leap from my map to the soft stones and hard rock that formed the Colorado River's other tributary canyons, chasms, creeks, cracks, gorges, gulches, narrows, meanders, and slots.

Olo, Matkatamiba, Havasupai—the names roll off the tongue. Lured by the legend of John D. Lee, I shouldered my pack and headed forty-two miles down the flood-scoured corridor of Buckskin Gulch–Paria Canyon with two friends. Called *Paria-Pa*, or "elk water," by the Kaibab Paiute, Paria Canyon and Buckskin Gulch formed one of the longest and narrowest canyons in the world. It was also one of the Grand Canyon's longest, deepest, and most rugged tributary chasms. Gouged by a sediment-bearing river that eroded a dark crack in the earth hundreds of feet deep at its head, Paria Canyon was more than three thousand feet deep at its confluence with the Colorado River below.

Heart of stone, Antelope Canyon

Trudging through mud, water, and quicksand, we followed the route of John D. Lee down the ancient Pueblo migration corridor for four days, through a canyon so narrow that it rarely saw sunlight. Here, Lee ramrodded one of the most audacious cattle drives in the annals of the West. "Called" by the Mormon Church to establish a ford across the Colorado River, Lee (a polygamist with eighteen wives) drove down fifty-four head of cattle through Paria Canyon in 1871. In reading his December 3 journal entry, I learned that we had had it easy: "We concluded to drive down the creek, which took us Some 8 days of toil, fatuige [sic], & labour, through brush, water, ice, & quick-sand & some time passing through narrow chasms with perpendicular Bluffs on both sides, some 3,000 feet high, & without seeing the sun for 48 hours."

Hard drives made hard men. But it was the tale of John D. Lee's lost gold that ignited talk around campfires throughout the West. The gold rush of 1849 still burned like firebrands in the minds of 550 men who struck down Kanab Creek two decades later.

That's what fired my imagination not long after emerging from the gray mud of Paria Canyon at Lees Ferry. I was lured by the prospect of seeing how Kanab Creek marked desperate men crazed with gold fever. I headed south from the Utah border one summer day and walked for four days toward the banks of the Colorado River below. Called a "creek" instead of a "canyon," Kanab Creek was deeper, more rugged, and 25 miles longer than Paria Canyon 142 river miles upstream.

Major Powell found that out when he ended his second Colorado River expedition at Kanab Creek on September 8, 1872. Fortunately, his cousin Clem wrote a letter to the *Chicago Tribune* describing the travails of the Kanab Creek gold rush:

> *Miners report every trail to the Colorado Cañons crowded with men seeking the new Eldorado . . . some come in wagons, some on horseback, muleback, afoot, and one in a donkey cart . . . The fever ran so high, that people crowded to the shore without food . . . After prospecting for a time, and getting but a few grains of fine gold, hopes fall, starvation stares them in the face.*

Not everyone who ventured through such rugged chasms lusted for gold. Some made sacred journeys. That's what called me down the Little Colorado River Gorge. I wanted to see the Hopi Salt Trail and trace the footsteps of Don Talayesva who made the pilgrimage in 1912. Battered by four days of hot sand and river cobble, I soaked my weary feet in the turquoise water, gazed at the blue sky and bronze cliffs floating overhead, and listened to his prayer: "Sun god, please . . . Direct our steps to Salt Canyon, and watch over us to return safely. Make our path smooth and renew our strength, so that our burden will be light."

I, too, needed strength to finish my journey, two sleeps beyond. I was alone, but I was not lonely. I was seeing a canyon few have known, but I was humbled in the presence of the silent stones. Native Americans call such places sacred. I understood why.

Hell Hole Bend, Little Colorado River Gorge

ABOVE: Cascades, Havasupai Indian Reservation

RIGHT: Flash flood, Shinumo Creek

Crack in the earth,
Buckskin Gulch–Paria
Canyon

Paria-Pa, Buckskin
Gulch–Paria Canyon

75

OPPOSITE: Last light,
Dead Indian Canyon
LEFT: Cathedral of stone,
Antelope Canyon

77

LEFT: Blue Springs, Little Colorado River Gorge
ABOVE: Flash flood, Thirty Mile Wash

Petroglyph, Nampaweap Canyon, Grand Canyon–Parashant National Monument

The Windows, Paria Canyon

"Show me the light." Buckskin Gulch–Paria Canyon

Emerald waters, Blue Springs,
Little Colorado River Gorge

84

Big Canyon,
Little Colorado River Gorge

Havasu Falls,
Havasupai Indian Reservation

Kanab Canyon,
Kanab Creek Wilderness–
Grand Canyon National Park

Petroglyphs, Nampaweap Canyon, Grand Canyon–Parashant National Monument

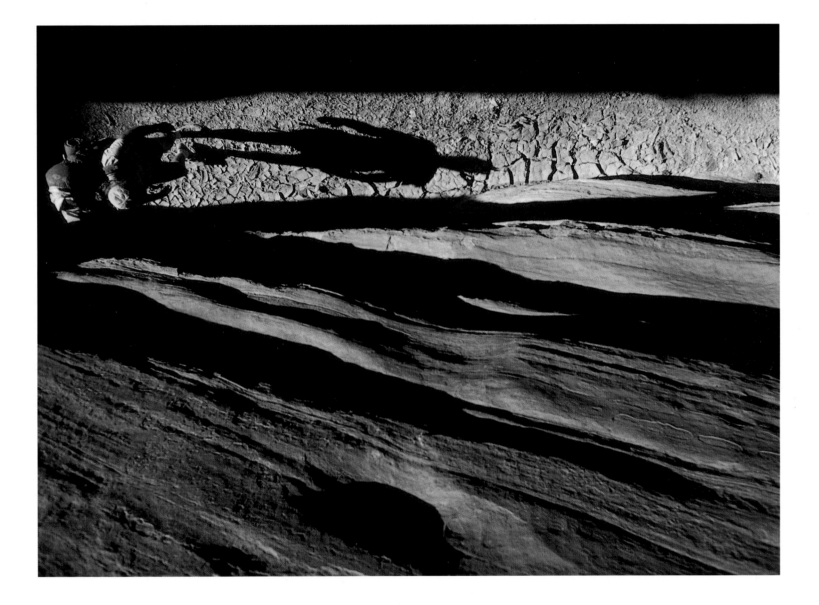

Corridor of stone, Buckskin Gulch–Paria Canyon

Bass's Camp, Shinumo Creek

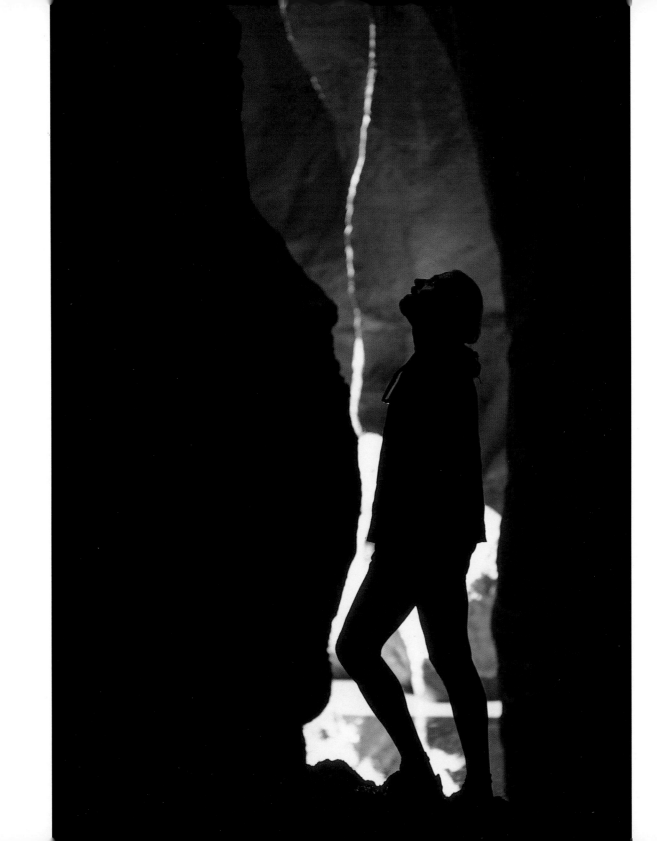

Wire Pass, Buckskin
Gulch–Paria Canyon

Salsipuedes,
"Get out if you can."
Buckskin Gulch–Paria Canyon

Quicksand, Buckskin Gulch–Paria Canyon

IV. RIVERS

ROMANCE OF THE COLORADO RIVER

Once in a lifetime, if one is lucky,
one so merges with sunlight and air and running water that
whole eons . . . might pass in a single afternoon.
—Loren Eiseley, 1946, The Immense Journey

I CLIMBED ECHO CLIFFS ONE BLUSTERY FALL DAY, stalked by the ghosts of black robes; in 1776 Domínguez and Escalante forged an escape route over the edge near here called *El Vado de Los Padres* ("The Crossing of the Fathers"). A reptilian fin of bloodred stone, Echo Cliffs offered a raven's view of Colorado River country I couldn't envision looking at a map. To the north, the twisting defile of Paria Canyon cleaved the Kaibito Plateau from the Paria like an ax blow. To the west, cloud-hugging, terra-cotta walls Major Powell called "vermilion" floated across a sagebrush sea to the verdant woods of the North Rim. At my feet, the muddy Colorado River writhed through the deep, dark fissure of Marble Canyon and disappeared into the thundering depths of the Great Unknown.

That's what Powell called the terrifying abyss below Marble Canyon during his first Colorado River expedition in 1869:

We are now ready to start on our way down the Great Unknown

. . . . We are three quarters of a mile in the depths of the earth, and the great river shrinks into insignificance as it dashes its angry waves against the walls and cliffs that rise to the world above; the waves are but puny ripples and we but pygmies, running up and down the sands or lost among the boulders . . . We have an unknown distance yet to run, an unknown river to explore. What falls there are, we know not; what rocks beset the channel, we know not; what walls rise above the river, we know not.

For years I longed to see the treacherous river Powell survived on bare-bones rations. I wanted to run the "awful" rapids that wrote the legends of a hundred other men and women who ran a wild river that, before 1950, was still "too thin to plow, and too thick to drink." And I wanted to feel the blisters, worn by hardwood oars, turn my palms to leather, my bones, chilled by icy water, warmed by hot wind burning my skin brown.

Opportunity finally knocked. On a river once thought to be the domain of men, a woman taught me how to run a river that killed thirty men before Bessie Hyde became the first woman to navigate the Colorado River during a honeymoon gone sour in 1928. That was eight years before Buzz Holstrom made the first solo run of the

Twilight, the Colorado, Carbon Creek

Grand Canyon in 1937, and then tried to tell women their place: "Women have their place in the world, but they do not belong in the Canyons of the Colorado."

So he thought. A woman showed me the river. Daybreak to nightfall for nearly a month, she showed me how to read the eddies, boils, whirlpools, currents, falls, riffles, holes, and big drops that formed 160 rapids that challenge 25,000 people every year. A woman introduced me to the 225-mile stretch of river that lashed the flotillas of adventurers who ran the mythic Colorado on outhouse lumber, flat-bottomed boats, sweep boats, canvas boats, bridge pontoons, G-rigs, J-rigs, snouts, sportyaks, kayaks, and paddle rafts.

Three weeks into my second trip on the water, I had a respite. Night fell and our tribe of river runners wandered off to cocoons among the rocks and scorpions. I laid out my sleeping bag on the paddle frame, as my boat tugged against the bowline, cradled back and forth by the river. I stared up at the window pinched between towering walls and wandered among the stars and comets that lit up the night sky. Birds sang shoreside, as currents murmured below. On the river, I'd become a prisoner of the Canyon, a prisoner of its beauty, a prisoner of its legends.

The explorations of Major Powell were the boldest brush strokes painted across Colorado River country's sweeping canvas. Others were just odd: What possessed the 1927 Clyde Eddy expedition to take a bear cub through the Grand Canyon? Others remain mysteries: Why did honeymooners Glen and Bessie Hyde disappear after piloting a wooden sweep boat nearly all the way through the

Canyon in 1928? And others were said to be Indian legend: Did Ti-Yo run the Colorado River in a hollowed-out canoe in his journey to the Hopi underworld?

Days later, I stood on the scalding black rocks overlooking Lava Falls. I was mesmerized by the tumbling white water that created one of the most feared rapids in North America. I was nervous plotting my first run through a take-no-prisoners Class 10 Big Drop that's challenged all comers, reduced some to tears, forced others to walk around, flipped hundreds, and dragged others helplessly down to the bottom of the river. I was also inspired. If legends are to be believed, and some are, prospector and horse thief James White may have been the "first man through" the Grand Canyon two years before Major Powell's maiden voyage. On September 7, 1867, the sunburned and emaciated White drifted up to the banks of Calville, Nevada, on a crude log raft, claiming he'd spent two weeks coming down the Big Cañon to escape hostile Ute Indians. What could Lava Falls possibly have been like for a man clinging to a log raft? I was about to take a bite.

As ritual demanded, I dunked my body into the cold river, cinched down my life jacket, and calmly assured my crew. Paddles dipped into the water. We eased our boat into the slick tongue. And suddenly we tipped over the edge of the world. "Forward!" I yelled. We dug our paddles in, plunging past a ledge hole that roared at us, and into the thunder that buried us. "Dig! Dig! Dig!" Our puny life raft buckled, twisted, and ran a booming wave train of exploding brown water that marked each of us forever.

Where rivers meet, confluence of the Colorado and Little Colorado

LEFT: Slow motion, House Rock Rapids
ABOVE: Against the wall, Crystal Rapids

Moonrise, the Colorado, Lees Ferry

RIGHT: Tapeats, the Colorado,
near Blacktail Canyon
OPPOSITE: Floating stone,
the Little Colorado,
Salt Trail Canyon

OPPOSITE: River foam, the Colorado, Carbon Creek

ABOVE: Mudflats, the Little Colorado

ABOVE: "The Great Unknown," the Colorado at Grapevine Creek

RIGHT: Smooth water, House Rock Rapids

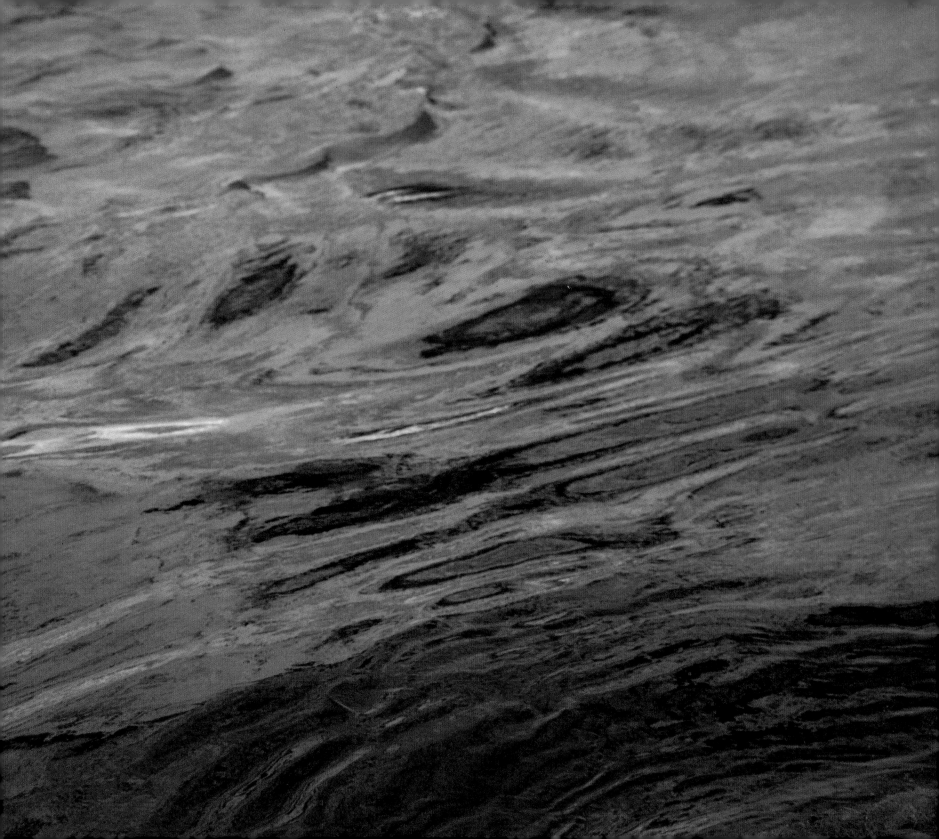

LEFT: Moonrise, the Colorado at Nankoweap Creek
ABOVE: Floating Marble Canyon Gorge

ABOVE: Anaasází granary, Middle Granite Gorge

OPPOSITE: Twilight, the Colorado, South Canyon

—

Enduring magic,
the Colorado near
Blacktail Canyon

Muddy waters, Hance Rapids

LEFT: The Colorado
near Travertine Canyon
OVERLEAF: Big Cañón,
the Colorado, Kanab Creek

115

OPPOSITE: Eye of the storm, Lava Falls

ABOVE: Day hiker, North Canyon

Boatwomen,
Clear Creek Falls

Salt Trail Canyon,
the Little Colorado

River to the Sea of Cortez: The Colorado,
Conquistador Aisle

ABOVE: River to the Sea of Cortez: The Colorado, Needles, California

RIGHT: The Colorado, U.S./Mexico border

OVERLEAF: Tidewater, where "the Grand Canyon empties into the Sea of Cortez"

124

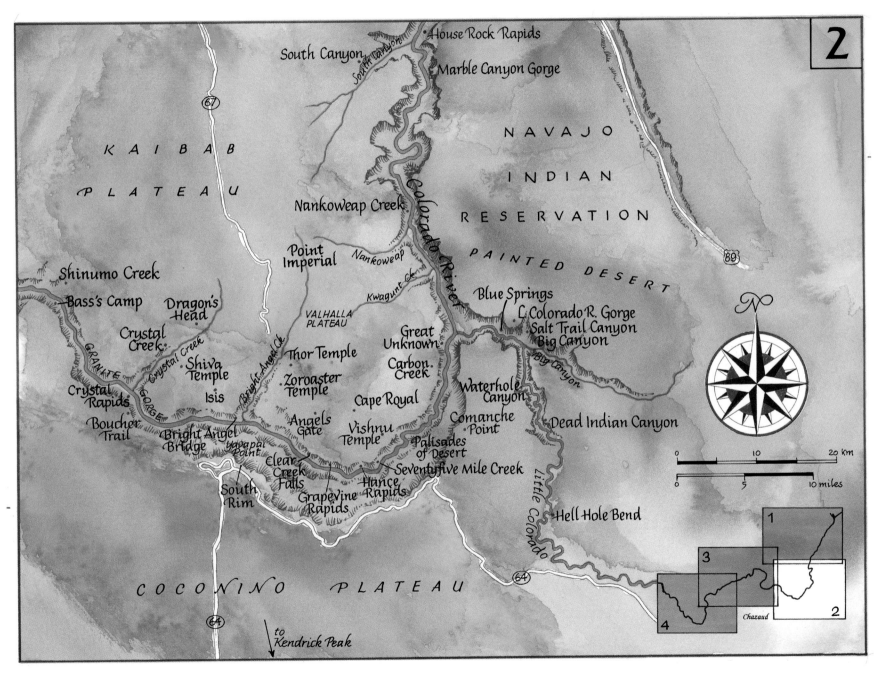

2

House Rock Rapids

South Canyon

South Canyon

Marble Canyon Gorge

67

N A V A J O

K A I B A B

I N D I A N

P L A T E A U

R E S E R V A T I O N

Nankoweap Creek

Colorado River

P A I N T E D   D E S E R T

89

Point
Imperial

Nankoweap

Shinumo Creek

Kwagunt Ck.

Blue Springs

Bass's Camp

Dragon's
Head

VALHALLA
PLATEAU

Great
Unknown

L. Colorado R. Gorge
Salt Trail Canyon
Big Canyon

Crystal
Creek

Crystal Creek

Thor Temple

Carbon
Creek

Big Canyon

Shiva
Temple

GRANITE

Bright Angel Ck.

Zoroaster
Temple

Waterhole
Canyon

Crystal
Rapids

Isis

Cape Royal

Comanche
Point

Dead Indian Canyon

Boucher
Trail

GORGE

Angels
Gate

Vishnu
Temple

Bright Angel
Bridge

Yavapai
Point

Palisades
of Desert

Clear
Creek
Falls

Seventyfive Mile Creek

South
Rim

Grapevine
Rapids

Hance
Rapids

Little Colorado

Hell Hole Bend

C O C O N I N O   P L A T E A U

64

64

to
Kendrick Peak

N

0   10   20 km

0   5   10 miles

1

3

2

4

Chazaud

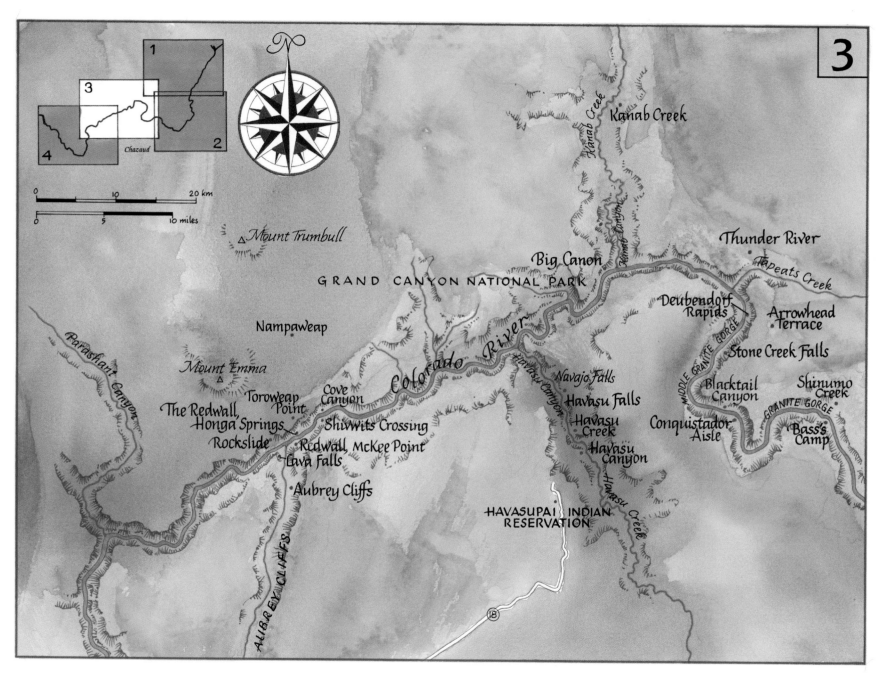

3

N

0   10   20 km
0   5   10 miles

Chazaud

Kanab Creek

Mount Trumbull

Thunder River

Big Canon

Tapeats Creek

GRAND CANYON NATIONAL PARK

Deubendorf Rapids

Arrowhead Terrace

Nampaweap

Colorado River

Stone Creek Falls

Parashant Canyon

Mount Emma

Navajo Falls

Blacktail Canyon

Shinumo Creek

Havasu Canyon

Havasu Falls

Toroweap Point

Cove Canyon

The Redwall

Honga Springs

Shivwits Crossing

Havasu Creek

Conquistador Aisle

Bass's Camp

Rockslide

Redwall McKee Point

Lava Falls

Havasu Canyon

MIDDLE GRANITE GORGE

GRANITE GORGE

Aubrey Cliffs

HAVASUPAI INDIAN RESERVATION

Havasu Creek

AUBREY CLIFFS

18

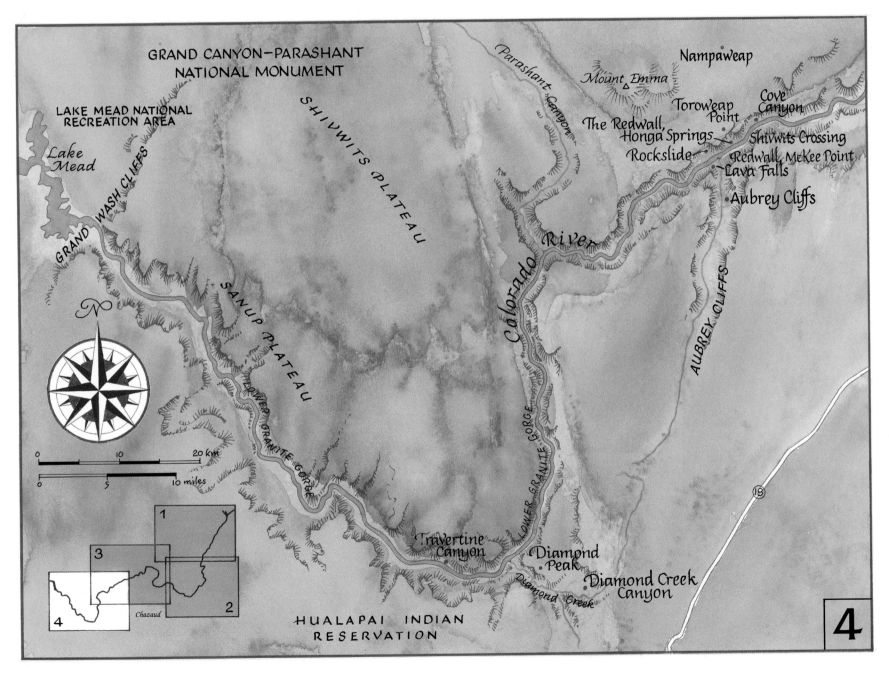

GRAND CANYON–PARASHANT
NATIONAL MONUMENT

LAKE MEAD NATIONAL
RECREATION AREA

SHIVWITS PLATEAU

Parashant Canyon

Nampaweap

Mount Emma

Toroweap Point

Cove Canyon

The Redwall,
Honga Springs

Shivwits Crossing

Rockslide

Redwall McKee Point
Lava Falls

Aubrey Cliffs

Lake Mead

GRAND WASH CLIFFS

Colorado River

SANUP PLATEAU

LOWER GRANITE GORGE

AUBREY CLIFFS

N

0   10   20 km

0   5   10 miles

18

1

3

2

4

Chazaud

Travertine Canyon

Diamond Peak

Diamond Creek

Diamond Creek Canyon

HUALAPAI INDIAN
RESERVATION

Notes to the Photographs

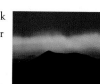 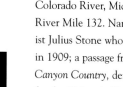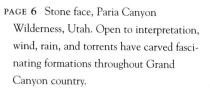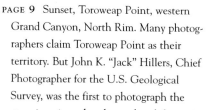

I. HORIZONS

PAGE 14 Dawn, Dead Horse Point State Park, Utah. The 5,680-foot Dead Horse Point overlooks Goose Neck of the Colorado River in Canyonlands National Park.

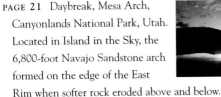

PAGE 17 Twilight, Delicate Arch, Arches National Park, Utah. Eroded over the last one hundred million years, this Entrada Sandstone landmark arch is the icon for the largest and most spectacular concentration of arches in the world. More than two thousand arches have been recorded here, from 3-foot windows to the 306-foot-wide Landscape Arch.

PAGE 18 Moonrise, Cliff Palace, Mesa Verde National Park, Colorado. Rediscovered by Richard Wetherill in 1888, Cliff Palace's 217 rooms and 23 *kivas* (ceremonial rooms) provided sanctuary for 250–350 pueblo-dwelling Anaasází (Navajo for "ancient ones") until they abandoned the area sometime during the thirteenth century.

PAGE 20 Rock mushrooms, Canyonlands National Park, Utah. Eons of wind, water, erosion, and uplift have sculpted intriguing landforms throughout Canyonlands, what Captain J. N. Macomb called "a worthless and impracticable region" when he explored it in 1859.

PAGE 21 Daybreak, Mesa Arch, Canyonlands National Park, Utah. Located in Island in the Sky, the 6,800-foot Navajo Sandstone arch formed on the edge of the East Rim when softer rock eroded above and below.

PAGE 22 Moonrise, Hovenweap Castle, Hovenweap National Monument, Utah. Scientists believe that eight hundred years ago the Anaasází aligned the windows of Hovenweap Castle for celestial observations in order to predict planting and harvest seasons.

PAGE 23 Square Tower House, Mesa Verde National Park, Colorado. The four-story Square Tower House, Cliff Palace, and four thousand other prehistoric sites in the area inspired President Theodore Roosevelt to sign legislation establishing Mesa Verde National Park on June 29, 1906.

PAGE 24 Sunrise, (left to right) 6,176-foot West Mitten Butte, 6,422-foot Sentinel Mesa, and 6,120-foot Big Indian, Monument Valley Navajo Tribal Park, Arizona. Many of the striking landforms in Monument Valley, and elsewhere throughout Navajo land, are sacred to traditional Navajo. *Álá Tsoh*, "Big Hands" or The Mittens, are said to be the hands of deities who will return.

PAGE 26 Fallen timbers, West Fork of Oak Creek, Arizona. A lush and rugged riparian corridor in the Red Rock Secret Mountain Wilderness, the fifteen-hundred-foot-deep West Fork of Oak Creek also drains the southern escarpment of the Colorado Plateau.

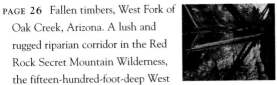

PAGE 27 Frijoles Falls, Rito de los Frijoles, Bandelier National Monument, New Mexico. Formed on the slopes of 10,199-foot Cerro Grande, the "Little River of Beans" is a tributary of the Upper Río Grande. *Rito*, or "rite," is an historic error in the translation and spelling of *rillíto*, which means "little river."

PAGE 28 Sunset, southern escarpment of the Colorado Plateau, Arizona. The Colorado Plateau encompasses 130,000 square miles; it includes the Four Corners region of Utah, Colorado, New Mexico, and Arizona. The seven-thousand-foot-high Mogollon Rim, a two-hundred-mile brink that stretches across central Arizona, forms its southern rim.

PAGE 30 Aerial view, Merrick Butte, Monument Valley Navajo Tribal Park, Arizona. Named for prospector James Merrick, who was killed nearby during the winter of 1879–80, 6,206-foot-high Merrick Butte is one of the few landforms in Monument Valley for which a traditional Navajo name is not widely known.

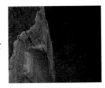

GRAND CANYON WILD

PAGE 31 Forested canyon, West Fork of Oak Creek, Arizona. Inspiration for Zane Grey's *The Call of the Canyon*, the area was described by the western writer: "only the murmuring stream broke the silence of the canyon."

PAGE 32 Caprock hoodoo, Grand Staircase–Escalante National Monument, Utah. A boulder tumbles from a cliff, and over eons the soft underlying layer of the Entrada Sandstone has eroded beneath the harder Dakota Formation, producing spectacular caprock hoodoos that defy belief at first sight.

PAGE 33 Red Rock Country, southern escarpment of the Colorado Plateau, Arizona. Called Hell's Hollow by cowboys and pioneer descendants who opposed national park status of Red Rock Country in the 1970s, Sedona's explosive growth and development no doubt has many old hands rolling over in their graves.

PAGE 34–35 Summer monsoon, Canyonlands National Park, Utah. Carved by wind, water, and erosion, Canyonlands receives two-thirds of its annual fifteen inches of precipitation during dramatic summer "monsoon" rains.

II. RIMS

PAGE 36 McKee Point, western Grand Canyon, South Rim. Edwin D. McKee came to the Grand Canyon in 1929, and earned a reputation as a park naturalist and geologist. The 6,280-foot McKee Point was named in honor of his legacy.

PAGE 38 Standing on the edge, Shiva Temple, North Rim. From the summit of 7,646-foot Shiva Temple, Craig Newman is dwarfed by the scale of what Theodore Roosevelt proclaimed in 1903 as "A natural wonder absolutely unparalleled throughout the rest of the world."

PAGE 40 The Colorado River from Toroweap Point, western Grand Canyon, North Rim. Looming 2,920 feet above the Colorado River at River Mile 177.5, 4,600-foot-high Toroweap Point provides one of the most remote and breathtaking vistas in North America.

PAGE 41 Rockslide, western Grand Canyon, North Rim. Formed around 300 million years ago, the Esplanade Formation is one the most captivating terraces to explore in the Grand Canyon.

PAGE 42 The Colorado, Lava Falls, western Grand Canyon. Located at River Mile 179.5, Lava Falls is America's most legendary rapids. When expedition leader Major John Wesley Powell portaged Lava Falls in 1869, he speculated on its cataclysmic origins: "What a conflict of water and fire there must have been here! Just imagine a river of molten rock running down into a river of melted snow. What a seething and boiling of waters; what clouds of steam rolled into the heavens!"

PAGE 43 Sunset, the Colorado River near Shivwits Crossing, western Grand Canyon, North Rim. This crossing was used by the Shivwits band of the Southern Paiute, who crossed the Colorado River at low water to trade with the Hualapai who lived on the south side of the river.

PAGE 44 Tyrolean traverse, Thunder River, North Rim. Rain and snow that fall on the North Rim percolate through the Kaibab Limestone and pool in subterranean aquifers, producing some of the Grand Canyon's most spectacular cataracts. Thunder River roars out of the Muav Limestone and forms a half-mile-long river that is arguably the shortest in the world.

PAGE 45 Marble Canyon, the Colorado River at Four Mile Wash, Glen Canyon National Recreation Area. For many, the Grand Canyon begins at the confluence of the Paria and Colorado Rivers at River Mile 1 and ends 279 miles downstream at Grapevine Wash, River Mile 280.

PAGE 46 Daybreak, East Rim of Vermilion Cliffs National Monument, Lees Ferry. A nesting area for California condors, the soaring walls of the 6,445-foot Vermilion Cliffs are comprised of multiple layers of sandstone and shale, including Navajo Sandstone, and the Kayenta, Moenave, Chinle, and Moenkopi Formations that give the rock its remarkable color.

PAGE 46–47 Tooth Rock, East Rim, Vermilion Cliffs National Monument, Lees Ferry. Towering 1,800 feet over the Colorado River at Marble Canyon, 6,139-foot-high Tooth Rock was first climbed on February 5, 1977, by Grand Canyon climbers George Bain, Spencer McIntyre, and Joe Sharber (ground support).

PAGE 47 Sundown, Echo Cliffs, Navajo Indian Reservation, Marble Canyon. Standing over Marble Canyon, the 5,496-foot Echo Cliffs are a Colorado River landmark, which Major Powell's men climbed on October 21, 1871. Firing a .44 Remington revolver from the 5,567-foot summit of Echo Peaks, Frederick S. Dellenbaugh wrote of the noise, saying that it was "a deafening shock like a thousand thunder-claps in one."

PAGE 48 Balanced Rock, Glen Canyon National Recreation Area, Lees Ferry. Comprised of Shinarump Conglomerate, this boulder toppled from the Vermilion Cliffs eons ago

and was left standing after the Moenkopi Formation eroded six feet beneath it.

PAGE 49 Horseshoe Bend, the Colorado River at Nine Mile Bar, Glen Canyon National Recreation Area. The only surviving stretch of Glen Canyon that wasn't flooded when Lake Powell filled with water in 1980 is the fifteen miles of quiet water that flows between Glen Canyon Dam and Lees Ferry at River Mile 0.

PAGE 50 First light, Angels Gate, North Rim. The 6,761-foot Angels Gate is remote and difficult to reach, but it is one of the most enticing of the Grand Canyon's temples to visit and photograph.

PAGE 51 Pioneer Grand Canyon climber Dave Ganci rappels from the summit of Angels Gate, North Rim. Like many of the canyon's most spectacular temples, Angels Gate is comprised of Coconino Sandstone that offers climbers rock that is relatively safe to climb in what Arizona climber Larry Trieber called a "great inverted mountain range."

PAGE 52–53 Skies of fire, Aubrey Cliffs, western Grand Canyon, South Rim. The 6,626-foot-high Aubrey Cliffs was named for plainsman Francis Xavier Aubrey, who is reputed to have won a $1,000 bet in 1850 and killed several horses to boot by riding more than

1,700 miles from Santa Fe, New Mexico, to Independence, Missouri, in eight days.

PAGE 54 The Redwall below McKee Point, western Grand Canyon, South Rim. Stained brilliant red from iron that runs off the upper layers, this 360-million-year-old geological formation was first named by Major Powell in 1869 when he said, "Storms have painted these limestones with pigment from above . . . Let it be called the red wall limestone."

PAGE 54 The Redwall at Honga Springs, western Grand Canyon, South Rim. From the days of the Anaasází, who wore yucca-fiber sandals, to the present, the 500- to 700-foot-high Redwall Limestone is the Canyon's most imposing barrier for foot travel.

PAGE 55 Petrified sand dunes, Paria Canyon–Vermilion Cliffs Wilderness, Arizona. At first glance, these colorful swirls in the Navajo Sandstone resemble ancient hand-painted pictographs.

PAGE 56 Wildfire sunset, Cape Royal, North Rim. Regional smog, including forest fires, emissions from coal-fired Navajo and Four Corners Power Plants, and pollutants from Los Angeles and Phoenix, mars visibility at the Grand Canyon for 90 percent of the time. On clearer days, 7,865-foot Cape Royal offers one of the best panoramic views of the Canyon.

PAGE 57 Petrified sand dunes, Paria Canyon–Vermilion Cliffs Wilderness, Arizona. These sedimentary bands of Navajo Sandstone appear to have the texture of fine-grained wood.

PAGE 58–59 Nightfall, East Rim, Vermilion Cliffs National Monument, Lees Ferry. Few places in Grand Canyon country are more enticing to roll out a bedroll than at the foot of these soaring black cliffs where echoes of the Colorado River soothe you to sleep.

PAGE 60–61 A climber's view, Peach Springs Canyon. Dave Ganci scrambles across the 3,512-foot-high summit of Diamond Peak, Hualapai Indian Reservation, South Rim. One arm quivering in a sling from a compound fracture, newspaperman Charles F. Lummis made an extraordinary ascent of 3,512-foot Diamond Peak in 1884 when he climbed it with his dog during a 40-mile detour from his 3,507-mile transcontinental walk from Cincinnati to Los Angeles.

PAGE 62 George Bain composes himself after a thirty-foot fall during the first ascent of the southwest face of Zoroaster Temple, North Rim. Named for the Persian deity, the 7,123-foot Zoroaster Temple was first climbed via its Northeast Arête by Dave Ganci and Arizonan Rick Tidrick on September 23, 1958.

PAGE 63 Twilight, Thor Temple, North Rim. Named for the Norse god, 6,719-foot-high Thor Temple was first climbed from the Wahalla Plateau solo by Alan Doty on May 14, 1977.

PAGE 64 Storm, Vishnu Temple, North Rim. Arguably the largest mountain in the Grand Canyon, the 7,529-foot-high Vishnu Temple was named after the Hindu god by geologist Clarence E. Dutton in 1880. Dutton wrote: "It is a gigantic butte, so admirably designed and so exquisitely decorated that the sight of it must call forth an expression of wonder and delight from the most apathetic beholder."

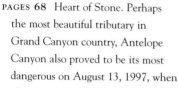

PAGE 65 Staring into an abyss, Shiva Temple, North Rim. From his precarious summit perch at 7,646 feet, George Bain peers into the depths of Trinity Creek. The 7,012-foot-high Isis is the twin-summited temple in the background.

PAGE 66 Rappeling, Comanche Point, East Rim. From 7,073-foot Comanche Point, the Colorado River at Tanner Rapids, River Mile 68.5, can be seen over four thousand vertical feet below.

PAGE 67–68 Comanche Point, Palisades of the Desert, East Rim. The western rim of the Painted Desert, Palisades of the Desert looms

over the Tanner Trail, an historic inner-canyon route used by the Hopi, Navajo, prospectors, moonshiners, and horse thieves during the late 1800s.

III. CHASMS

PAGES 68 Heart of Stone. Perhaps the most beautiful tributary in Grand Canyon country, Antelope Canyon also proved to be its most dangerous on August 13, 1997, when eleven canyoneers drowned in a flash flood after ignoring storm warnings of local Navajo.

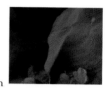

PAGE 71 Hell Hole Bend, Little Colorado River Gorge, Navajo Indian Reservation. During his 1869 expedition down the Colorado, Major Powell compared the Little Colorado River Gorge to the Grand Canyon: "The Colorado Chiquito . . . enters through a canyon on a scale quite as grand as that of the Colorado itself." Returning from measuring the gorge's three-thousand-foot-high walls, with barometer readings the next day, Powell added: "The impression is given that we are at great depths, and we look up to see but a little patch of sky."

PAGE 72 Cascades, Havasupai Indian Reservation, South Rim. The spiritual and economic lifeblood of the Havasupai, Havasu Creek attracts visitors from all over the world to marvel at its waters.

PAGE 73 Flash flood, Shinumo
Creek, North Rim. Ancestral lands
of the Shivwits band of Southern
Paiute, *Shinumo* is said to mean
"cliff dwellers" or "old ones."

PAGE 74 Crack in the earth, Buckskin
Gulch–Paria Canyon Wilderness, Utah.
Hundreds of feet deep, and frequently no
more than fifteen feet wide, Buckskin
Gulch is a twelve-mile-long tributary of
Paria Canyon that resembles a gash in the
earth more than it does the popular notion of a canyon.

PAGE 75 Paria-Pa, Buckskin Gulch–
Paria Canyon Wilderness, Utah. Called
Paria-Pa, or "elk water," by the Kaibab
band of the Southern Paiute who used
the ancient Pueblo migration corridor,
Buckskin Gulch–Paria Canyon; called an
"inclosed meander" by geologists for the narrow, close-set
180-degree turns the river cut through the Navajo
Sandstone.

PAGE 76 Last light, Dead Indian
Canyon, Little Colorado River
Gorge, Navajo Indian Reservation.
Sixty-one river miles downstream
from the confluence of the Paria
and Colorado Rivers, the 57-mile-long, 4,024-foot-deep
Little Colorado River Gorge forms the Grand Canyon's
deepest tributary canyon.

PAGE 77 Antelope Canyon, a cathedral
of stone, was carved by flash floods that
have swept down from six-thousand-
foot-high Kaibito Plateau.

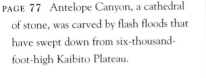

PAGE 78 Blue Springs, Little Colorado
River Gorge, Navajo Indian
Reservation. Vibrant blue from
copper sulfate and calcium carbon-
ate, Blue Springs water is nearly
unpalatable to drink in spite of its
alluring color.

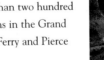

PAGE 79 Flash flood, Thirty Mile Wash,
Marble Canyon. Such violent forces of
nature have cut more than two hundred
named tributary canyons in the Grand
Canyon between Lees Ferry and Pierce
Ferry.

PAGE 80 Petroglyph, Nampaweap
Canyon, Grand Canyon–
Parashant National Monument,
Arizona. Ceremonial dancer?
Evil spirit? Only speculation can
define the meaning of this ancient drawing pecked into
black basalt.

PAGE 81 The Windows, Paria
Canyon Wilderness, Utah. Eroded
into Navajo Sandstone, the
Windows' alcoves, caves, and
chambers are an enticing destina-
tion for day hikers and photographers.

PAGE 82–83 "Show me the light,"
Buckskin Gulch–Paria Canyon
Wilderness, Utah and Arizona. The
fleeting warmth and luminescent
beauty of sunlight is refracted off
water-sculpted walls above canyoneer Richard Nobeker.

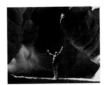

PAGE 84 Emerald waters, Blue Springs,
Little Colorado River Gorge, Navajo
Indian Reservation. Twenty-five thousand
river runners raft the Colorado each year;
the high point for many is a swim in the
emerald waters of the Little Colorado
River.

PAGE 85 Big Canyon, Little Colorado River
Gorge, Navajo Indian Reservation. Called
Tótchi' íkooh, "Red Water Canyon," by the
Navajo and *Colorado Chiquito*, "Little
Red River," by Major Powell, the Little
Colorado River Gorge is known by a vari-
ety of other names given by river runners, including LC,
LCR, and the Little C.

PAGE 86 Havasu Falls, Havasupai Indian
Reservation, South Rim. Derived from
Havasupai, or "People of the Blue-green
water," Havasu Falls lured prospectors during the 1870s to mine the homeland para-
dise of the last remaining canyon-dwelling
Native Americans.

PAGE 87 Kanab Canyon, Kanab Creek Wilderness–Grand Canyon National Park, North Rim. Rivaling the Little Colorado River Gorge eighty-two river miles upstream, Kanab Creek is fifty-seven miles long and 3,892 feet deep. The gold rush of 1871–82 lured more than five hundred prospectors down the length of Kanab Creek in quest for gold, which was rumored to be ripe for the plucking in the sands of the Colorado River.

PAGE 88 Petroglyphs, Nampaweap Canyon, Grand Canyon–Parashant National Monument. Said to mean "foot-canyon" in Paiute, *Nampaweap* boasts one of the largest concentrations of prehistoric rock drawings in the region. These date back ten thousand years.

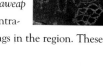

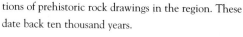

PAGE 89 Corridor of stone, Buckskin Gulch–Paria Canyon Wilderness, UT and AZ. Corrasion is a process in which sediment-bearing, flood-swollen creeks cut through a stratum of soft sandstone to form the region's corridors of stone.

PAGE 90 Bass's Camp, Shinumo Creek, North Rim. Established by William Wallace Bass in 1887, Bass used his Shinumo Creek camp as a base to mine asbestos, tend an orchard, and as a waystation for tourists. In *The Grand Canyon of Arizona*, nineteenth-century travel writer George Wharton James wrote, "Another two or three weeks' delightful experience can be gained by arranging

to go down Bass Trail, cross on his cable ferry, go up the Shinumo Trail to Powell Plateau, [and] watch herds of protected and preserved deer and antelope."

PAGE 91 Wire Pass, Buckskin Gulch–Paria Canyon Wilderness, Utah and Arizona. Popularly known by canyoneers such as Richard Nebeker as "narrows" and "slot canyons," geologist Herbert E. Gregory first described these sinuous canyons as "inclosed meanders" when he surveyed the desolate 5,400-square-mile Kaiparowits Plateau on a pack mule in 1915.

PAGE 92 *Salsipuedes*, "Get out if you can." Buckskin Gulch–Paria Canyon Wilderness, Utah and Arizona. Trapped at the foot of Echo Cliffs and the mouth of Paria Canyon, Spanish padres Francisco Atanasio Domínguez and Silvestre Vélez de Escalante coined a phrase on October 26, 1776, that still resonates with canyoneer Richard Nebeker more than two hundred years later.

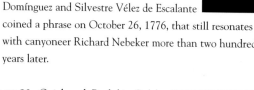
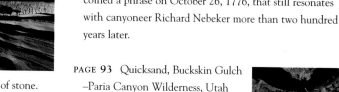

PAGE 93 Quicksand, Buckskin Gulch–Paria Canyon Wilderness, Utah and Arizona. A legend of the Old West, "quicksand" was popularized in the heyday of cinematic cowboys. Though troublesome for John Wayne and John D. Lee's cattle, canyoneers have to work at trying not to sink more than knee-deep in Paria's silt-borne muck.

IV. RIVERS

PAGE 94 Twilight, the Colorado River at Carbon Creek. River Mile 64.5. "How deep is the river?" is one of the most frequently asked questions by river runners. Average depth ranges from thirty-five to eighty-five feet.

PAGE 97 Where rivers meet, the confluence of the Colorado and the Little Colorado Rivers. River Mile 61.5. Major Powell called the mother river the Rio Colorado and its tributary the Colorado Chiquito. Both names date back to 1699 when Padre Eusebio Francisco Kino's diarist, Lt. Juan Mateo Manje (Mange), first called it the "true Río del Norte of the ancients . . . the fertile Río Colorado."

PAGE 98 Slow motion, House Rock Rapids, Marble Canyon. River Mile 17. A seventeen-year-old member of Powell's 1871 expedition, poet laureate of high adventure Frederick S. Dellenbaugh described how House Rock Rapids was named in his 1908 book *A Canyon Voyage: The Narrative of the Second Powell Expedition*: "About sunset we passed two large boulders which had fallen together, forming a rude shelter, under which Riggs or someone else had slept, and then jocosely printed above with charcoal the words 'House Rock Hotel'."

PAGE 99 Against the wall, Louise Teal runs the left side of Crystal Rapids, Upper Granite Gorge.

Located at River Mile 98, Crystal Rapids is one of the most dangerous rapids in North America. Five river runners died in Crystal Rapids during the 1980s–90s, and they were wearing Class IV life jackets.

PAGE 100–101   Moonrise, the Colorado River at Lees Ferry, Glen Canyon National Recreation Area. Named for Mormon polygamist, farmer, and prospector John D. Lee, who established the first reliable ford across the Colorado at River Mile 0 on January 18, 1872. Fifty-one years later, the U.S. Geological Survey instituted the practice of measuring river mileages downstream from Lees Ferry during the 1923 Claude Birdseye expedition.

PAGE 102   Tapeats, the Colorado River near Blacktail Canyon, Conquistador Aisle. Named for *Tumpeats*, or "Small Rocks," Major Powell's Paiute guide, the 545-million-year-old Tapeats Sandstone forms the beautiful outer rim of the Tonto Formation and Inner Gorge near River Mile 121.

PAGE 103   Floating stone, Little Colorado River, Salt Trail Canyon, Navajo Indian Reservation. Before entering Salt Trail Canyon during his first salt pilgrimage in 1912, Third

Mesa Hopi Don Talayesva prayed for a safe journey: "Sun god, please notice that I have carved my clan emblem upon the stone. Direct our steps to Salt Canyon, and watch over us until we return safely. Make our path smooth and renew our strength, so that our burden will be light."

PAGE 104   River foam, the Colorado River at Carbon Creek. River Mile 64.5. Recharged with monsoon runoff from the Little Colorado River, the Colorado River carried an

average of 168 million tons of silt each year before construction of Glen Canyon Dam dramatically changed its character to a clear, cold river.

PAGE 105   Mudflats, Little Colorado River, Navajo Indian Reservation. Coyotes also fall victim to flash floods that periodically sweep down narrow chasms like the

Little Colorado River Gorge. On August 7, 2001, a flash flood claimed the lives of two veteran canyoneers in the gorge.

PAGE 106   "The Great Unknown," the Colorado River at Grapevine Creek, Upper Granite Gorge. River Mile 81.5. Emerging from Marble Canyon during his 1869 expedition, Major Powell entered

what he feared was the Great Unknown on August 13: "We are now ready to start on our way down the Great Unknown."

PAGE 107   Smooth water, the Colorado River at House Rock Rapids, Marble Canyon. River Mile 17. The Colorado River's average temperature today is forty-eight

degrees Fahrenheit compared with its eighty-degree average before the completion of Glen Canyon Dam in 1964.

PAGE 108   Moonrise, the Colorado River at Nankoweap Creek, Marble Canyon. River Mile 52.5. Anglicized from *ninkoipi*, or "people killed," the oral history of the Kaibab band of

Southern Paiute recounts the tragic nighttime massacre of Kaibab by "Apaches" above the Colorado River in Nankoweap Creek.

PAGE 109   Floating Marble Canyon Gorge. River Mile 35. Major Powell described Marble Canyon's majestic scenery on August 9, 1869: "And now the scenery is on a grand scale. The walls of the canyon, 2,500 feet high, are of marble, of many

beautiful colors, often polished below by the waves, and sometimes far up the side where showers have washed over the cliffs."

PAGES 110   Anaasází granary, above the Colorado River, Middle Granite Gorge. River Mile 132. Used for scale, sunglasses show the small stone structures prehistoric Pueblo

people used to store clay *ollas* (pots) of corn, piñón nuts, and water.

PAGE 111   Twilight, the Colorado River at South Canyon, Marble Canyon. River Mile 31.5. Unequipped with life jackets, three men drowned and Robert Brewster Stanton aborted his first 1889 expedition at South Canyon to survey a river-level railroad through the Grand Canyon.

PAGE **112–113** Enduring magic, the Colorado River near Blacktail Canyon, Conquistador Aisle. Stretching from River Mile 120 to 123 at the head of the Middle  Granite Gorge, this river corridor was known as Alarcon Aisle and Explorers Canyon until the United States Board on Geographic Names officially named it Conquistador Aisle in 1906.

PAGE **114** Muddy waters, the Colorado River at Hance Rapids, Upper Granite Gorge. River Mile 76.5. During the heyday of Colorado River exploration, its 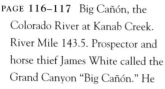 muddy waters were said to be "too thin to plow and too thick to drink."

PAGE **115** The Colorado River near Travertine Canyon, Lower Granite Gorge, Hualapai Indian Reservation. River Mile 130. These are the ancestral lands of the Hualapai and Shivwits band of Southern Paiute; both groups of indigenous canyon dwellers were known to cross the river on rafts for trade and warfare.

PAGE **116–117** Big Cañon, the Colorado River at Kanab Creek. River Mile 143.5. Prospector and  horse thief James White called the Grand Canyon "Big Cañon." He may have navigated the Grand Canyon on a log raft two years before Powell's 1869 maiden voyage. Powell ended his second Colorado River expedition at Kanab Creek in 1872 when he said to his crew, "Well, boys, our voyage is done!"

PAGE **118** Eye of the storm, Lava Falls. River Mile 179.5. Few 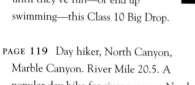 river runners can rightfully claim they've rafted the Grand Canyon until they've run—or end up swimming—this Class 10 Big Drop.

PAGE **119** Day hiker, North Canyon, Marble Canyon. River Mile 20.5. A popular day hike for river runners, North 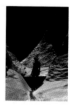 Canyon's flash floods created a rapid at the head of a ten-mile stretch of rapids in Marble Canyon called the Roaring Twenties.

PAGE **120** Boatwomen Louise Teal (left) and Ginger Henchman, Clear Creek Falls at River Mile 84.

PAGE **121** Salt Trail Canyon, Little Colorado River, Navajo Indian Reservation. Named for Hopi salt 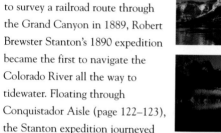 pilgrimages, the Little Colorado River Gorge was also visited by the Havasupai who roasted mescal hearts from agave collected in the depths of the canyon.

PAGES **122–127** River to the Sea of Cortez. After his failed attempt to survey a railroad route through the Grand Canyon in 1889, Robert Brewster Stanton's 1890 expedition became the first to navigate the Colorado River all the way to tidewater. Floating through Conquistador Aisle (page 122–123), the Stanton expedition journeyed down the Colorado River below the Grand Canyon, past Needles, California (page 124), toward the United States/Mexico border (page 125), to the Gulf of California (page 126–127) where the "Grand Canyon empties into the Sea of Cortez." The journey was not repeated until 1911–12 when Grand Canyon explorers and 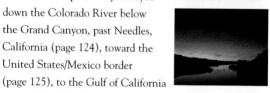  photographers Ellsworth and Emery Kolb memorialized their adventure with the "first motion picture" and the 1914 book *Through the Grand Canyon from Wyoming to Mexico.*

SELECTIVE BIBLIOGRAPHY

Annerino, John. *Adventuring in Arizona*. San Francisco: Sierra Club Books, 1991; revised edition 1996; University of Arizona Press edition 2003.

___. *Canyons of the Southwest*, (photographs by the author), cloth. San Francisco: Sierra Club Books, 1993. University of Arizona Press (paperback) 2000.

___. *Hiking the Grand Canyon, A Sierra Club Totebook*. San Francisco: Sierra Club Books, 1986, revised edition (with a Fold-out Trail Map by the author), 1993.

___. *People of Legend: Native Americans of the Southwest*, (photographs by the author), cloth. San Francisco: Sierra Club Books, 1996.

___. *Running Wild: An Extraordinary Adventure of the Human Spirit*. New York: Marlowe & Co., 1998.

___. *Running Wild: Through the Grand Canyon on the Ancient Path*. Tucson and London: Harbinger House, 1992.

___. "Grand Canyon Climbs." *Mountain*, Number 77 (January/ February 1981): 25–35. [England]

Bailey, Paul. *Jacob Hamblin: Buckskin Apostle*. Los Angeles: Western Lore, 1948.

Bain, George. Personal communication, 2003.

Bandelier, Adolph A. *The Delight Makers: A Novel of Prehistoric Pueblo Indians*. New York: Dodd, Mead, 1890.

Bartlett, Katharine. "How Don Pedro de Tovar Discovered the Hopi and Don García López de Cárdenas Saw the Grand Canyon, with Notes Upon Their Probable Route." *Plateau*, vol. 12, no. 3 (January 1940): 35–45.

Belknap, Buzz and Loie Belknap Evans. *Grand Canyon River Guide*. Evergreen, CO: Westwater Books, 2001.

Bolton, Herbert E. *Pageant in the Wilderness: The Story of the Escalante Expedition to the Interior Basin, 1776. Including the Diary and Itinerary of Father Escalante Translated and Annotated*. Salt Lake City: Utah Historical Society, 1950.

Brian, Nancy. *River to Rim: A Guide to Place Names Along the Colorado River in Grand Canyon from Lake Powell to Lake Mead*. Flagstaff, AZ: Earthquest Press, 1992.

Brooks, Juanita, and Robert Glass Cleland, eds. *A Mormon Chronicle: The Diaries of John D. Lee, 1848–1876, Volume II*. Salt Lake City: University of Utah Press, 1983.

Carmony, Neil B., ed. "The Grand Canyon Deer Drive of 1924, The Accounts of Will C. Barnes and Mark E. Musgrave." *The Journal of Arizona History*, vol. 43, no.1 (Spring 2002): 41–64.

Corle, Edwin. *Listen Bright Angel*. New York: Duell, Sloan & Pearce, 1946.

Coues, Elliot. *On the Trail of a Spanish Pioneer: The Diary and Itinerary of Francisco Garcés (Missionary Priest) in His Travels Through Sonora, Arizona, and California, 1775–1776; Translated from an Official Contemporaneous Copy of the Original Spanish Manuscript, and edited, with Copious Critical Notes by Elliot Coues*. 2 vols. New York: Francis P. Harper, 1900.

Crampton, C. Gregory. *Land of Living Rock: The Grand Canyon and the High Plateaus: Arizona, Utah, Nevada*. New York: Alfred A. Knopf, 1972.

___. *Standing Up Country: The Canyon Lands of Utah and Arizona*. New York and Salt Lake City: Alfred A. Knopf and University of Utah Press in Association with the Amon Carter Museum of Western Art, 1964.

Dawson, Thomas F. *The Grand Canyon, An Article: Giving the Credit of First Traversing the Grand Canyon of the Colorado to James White, A Colorado Gold Prospector, Who it is Claimed Made the Voyage Two Years Previous to the Expedition Under the Direction of Maj. J.W. Powell in 1869*. 65th Congress, 1st Session, Senate Resolution No. 79, June 4, 1917, Document No. 42. Washington, DC: U.S. Government Printing Office, 1917.

Dellenbaugh, Frederick S. *A Canyon Voyage: The Narrative of the Second Powell Expedition Down the Green-Colorado River from Wyoming, and the Exploration on Land, in the Years 1871 and 1872*. New York: Putnam, 1908.

Dutton, Clarence Edward. *Tertiary History of the Grand Canyon District, with Atlas*. Department of Interior Monographs of the United States Geological Survey, vol. 2. Washington, DC: U.S. Government Printing Office, 1882.

Eiseley, Loren. *The Immense Journey: An Imaginative Naturalist Explores the Mysteries of Man and Nature*. New York: Random House, 1946.

Fewkes, J. Walter. "The Snake Cermonies at Walpi." *A Journal of American Ethnology and Archaeology*, vol. 4, 1894.

Flavell, George F. *The Log of the Panthon: An Account of an 1896 River Voyage from Green River, Wyoming to Yuma, Arizona through the Grand Canyon*. Edited by Neil B. Carmony and David E. Brown. Boulder, CO: Pruett, 1987.

Granger, Byrd H. *Grand Canyon Place Names*. Tucson: University of Arizona Press, 1960.

Gregory, Herbert Ernest, and Robert C. Moore. *The Kaiparowits Region: A Geographic and Geologic Reconnaissance of Parts of Utah and Arizona*. Washington, DC: U.S. Government Printing Office, 1931.

Grey, Zane. *The Call of the Canyon*. New York: Grosset & Dunlap, 1924.

Hughes, J. Donald. *In the House of Stone and Light: A Human*

History of the Grand Canyon. Grand Canyon, AZ: Grand Canyon Natural History Association, 1978.

___. *The Story of Man at the Grand Canyon*. Grand Canyon, AZ: Grand Canyon Natural History Association, 1967.

James, George Wharton. *In and Around the Grand Canyon: The Grand Canyon of the Colorado River in Arizona*. Boston: Little, Brown & Co., 1900.

___. *The Grand Canyon of Arizona: How to See It*. Boston: Little, Brown & Co., 1905.

Kelly, Isabel Truesdell, and Catherine S. Fowler. "Southern Paiute." In *Handbook of North American Indians: Great Basin, Volume 11*. Washington, DC: Smithsonian Institution, 1986.

Kolb, Ellsworth L. *Through the Grand Canyon from Wyoming to Mexico*. New York: McMillan, 1914.

Lavender, David. *River Runners of the Grand Canyon*. Grand Canyon and Tucson: Grand Canyon Natural History Association and University of Arizona Press, 1985.

Linford, Laurance D. *Navajo Places: History, Legend, Landscape*. Salt Lake City: University of Utah Press, 2000.

Lummis, Charles Fletcher. *A Tramp Across the Continent*. New York: Charles Scribner's Sons, 1892.

Ortiz, Alfonso, ed. *Handbook of North American Indians: Southwest, Volume 9*. Washington, DC: Smithsonian Institution, 1979.

___. *Handbook of North American Indians: Southwest, Volume 10*. Washington, DC: Smithsonian Institution, 1983.

Powell, J. W. *The Exploration of the Colorado River and Its Canyons*. New York: Dover Publications, 1961.

___. *An Overland Trip to the Grand Canyon*. Palmer Lake, CO: Filter Press, 1974.

Powell, Walter Clement. "Journal of Walter Clement Powell." Edited by Charles Kelly. *Utah Historical Quarterly*, vols. 16–17 (1948–49): 257–478.

Reisner, Marc. *Cadillac Desert: The American West and Its Disappearing Water*. New York: Penguin Books, 1986.

Roosevelt, Theodore. New York *Sun*, May 7, 1903.

___. *A Book-Lover's Holidays in the Open*. New York: Charles Scribner's Sons, 1916.

Rusho, W. L., and C. Gregory Crampton. *Desert River Crossing: Historic Lee's Ferry on the Colorado River*. Salt Lake City: Peregrine Smith, 1981.

Stanton, Robert Brewster. *Down the Colorado River*. Edited by Dwight L. Smith. Norman: University of Oklahoma Press, 1965.

Stevens, Larry. *The Colorado River in Grand Canyon: A Comprehensive Guide to Its Natural and Human History*. Flagstaff, AZ: Red Lake Books, 1999.

Stone, Julius Frederick. *Canyon Country: The Romance of a Drop of Water and a Grain of Sand*. New York: G.P. Putnam's Sons, 1932.

Talayesva, Don C. *Sun Chief: The Autobiography of a Hopi Indian*. Edited by Leo W. Simmons. New Haven, CT, and London: Yale University Press, 1948.

Teal, Louise. *Breaking into the Current: Boatwomen of the Grand Canyon*. Tucson and London: University of Arizona Press, 1994.

Van Valkenburgh, Richard F., and Clyde Kluckhorn, eds. *Navajo Sacred Places*. New York: Garland Publishing, 1974.

LITERATURE CITED

p. 7 Theodore Roosevelt. New York *Sun*, May 7, 1903.

p. 12 "You cannot see the Grand Canyon . . ."; J. W. Powell. *The Exploration of the Colorado River and Its Canyons*. New York: Dover Publications, 1961, p. 397.

p. 15 C. Gregory Crampton. *Land of Living Rock: The Grand Canyon and the High Plateaus: Arizona, Utah, Nevada*. New York: Alfred A. Knopf, 1972, pp. 17, 3.

p. 16 "These Indians put me to shame"; J. W. Powell. *An Overland Trip to the Grand Canyon*. Palmer Lake, CO: Filter Press, 1974, p. 14.

p. 16 "Wild majestic cliffs loomed taller . . ."; Charles Fletcher Lummis. *A Tramp Across the Continent*. New York: Charles Scribner's Sons, 1892, p. 242.

p. 37 Theodore Roosevelt. *A Book-Lover's Holidays in the Open*. New York: Charles Scribner's Sons, 1916, p. 1.

p. 39 A hermit who "wore a white beard and white mustache [while] jogging along on his white mule"; Edwin Corle. *Listen Bright Angel*. New York: Duell, Sloan & Pearce, 1967, p. 45.

p. 69 Don C. Talayesva, *Sun Chief: The Autobiography of a Hopi Indian*. Edited by Leo W. Simmons. New Haven, CT, and London: Yale University Press, 1948, p. 288.

p. 70 "We concluded to drive down the . . ."; Juanita Brooks and Robert Glass Cleland, eds. *A Mormon Chronicle: The Diaries of John D. Lee, 1848–1876*, Volume II. Salt Lake City: University of Utah Press, 1983, p. 178.

p. 70 "Miners report every trail . . ."; Walter Clement Powell. "Journal of Walter Clement Powell." Edited by Charles Kelley. *Utah Historical Quarterly*, volumes 16–17 (1948–49): 402–403.

p. 70 "Sun god, please . . ."; Talayesva, p. 235.

p. 95 Loren Eiseley. *The Immense Journey*. New York: Random House, 1946, p. 16.

p. 95 "We are now ready to start on our way down the Great Unknown." J. W. Powell. p. 248.

p. 95 "Too thin to plow, and too thick to drink"; J. Donald Hughes. *The Story of Man at the Grand Canyon*. Grand Canyon, AZ: Grand Canyon Natural History Association, 1967, p. 45.

p. 96 "Women have their place in the world . . ."; David Lavender. *River Runners of the Grand Canyon*. Grand Canyon and Tucson: Grand Canyon Natural History Association and University of Arizona Press, 1985, p. 94.

**Embraced by stone,
Buckskin Gulch–Paria Canyon**